Latitude, Longitude

Latitude, Longitude

Poems by

Nancy Anne Miller

Cover design by Shay Culligan

ISBN: 978-1-954353-32-9

Kelsay Books
502 South 1040 East, A-119
American Fork, Utah, 84003

To Kim, Marsha, Wendy, my Bermudian poet and artist friends, who also live abroad and are inspired by their beloved island.

Perhaps if you remain you will become civilized,
detached, refined, your words pruned of lush.
Lush is an indictment in this lean place
where all things thin are judged best.
What to do then with the bush and jungle
sprouting from your pen?
—Lorna Goodison

The hurricane does not roar in pentameter.
—Edward Kamau Brathwaite

Mi dear, times hard
but things lush-lush here
on this piece of stream
of conscious landscape -
this wilful Eden trod on by every race.
—Grace Nichols

Acknowledgments

I would like to thank the editors of the following journals for publishing the following poems.

Adda: The Commonwealth Journal of Writing (UK): "Polar," "Hurricane Humberto"

Caribbean Quarterly(JA): "Ode to Sappho," "Walcott's Lament"

Moko (BVI): "Sun Spots"

A New Ulster (IE): "Pitch," "Neither," "No One Here to Tell," "No One Visits," "Tooth Fairy," "Envelope"

Orbis(GB): "Gravestones," "Effigy"

PREE (JA): "Straw," "Secret Society"

The Punch Magazine (IN): "Pink Wall Clock," "Inner Tube," "Sun Prayers," "Island Wave," "Good Friday Kite"

Sargasso: A Journal of Caribbean Literature, Language and Culture (PR): "Jigsaw," "House of Mirrors," "Winter Survival"

SurVision Magazine: (IE): "Leonora's Landscape," "The Poem is Here"

sx salon(CAR): "Immense and Clumsy," "Long Tale"

Contents

Latitude, Longitude

No One Here to Tell

Sun Spots

Ode to Sappho

Thank you for leaving fragments,
'the shards of language' as Walcott says,
like what falls away from a poem
and is not understood, a few lines,
fragment of memory, ghostly as a ship
wreck broken apart in tropical seas.

Thank you for leaving fragments,
a phrase, the poem's true meaning,
not just the part it plays: the anole
lizard's dewlap flashing into
an orange bud, the cereus
blooming within its one night.

Thank you for leaving fragments,
I am exiled from my past, poems
piece meal, ocean drenched ruins,
random mollusk shells I collect,
sea surfaced, shattered, momentarily
brighten the tide's curving line.

Walcott's Lament

Said off island, he became
disoriented. I, too, miss
the sea's rocking back, forth.
I'm a metronome, keep its time.

The spasmic white surf
girdling the land, holds
it in tight, shrinks me into
a landscape, I fit. Queen Palms

turn the sky into a vaulted
Gothic ceiling, like it too wants
mooring, to remain in place,
above the ocean's shifting blue.

Poetry is an Island

Like china from England, the Continent:
Spode, Limoges, Meissen, tectonic plates

are fragile, break as Walcott said, "Poetry is
an Island broken off from the main."

Bermuda so formed, balances on a volcano,
the sea's fingers steady while the tide crashes

in brittle sounds: a tea tray of pots, cups smashed,
picked up by the next wave's hand. How fragile

each day adrift is. Time has steadied us here,
protects us with the reefs' levies where Parrotfish

float, chips from a Wedgewood plate, scatter
the seafloor with porous limestone on which we rest.

Ocean crushed shells, fine grained and soft, make us
pink with pride, coral sands blush our contentment.

Bull in a China Shop

The singular Spode, Limoges,
Meissen plates at Bluck's China
stick up in transparent cases

like shells in an aquarium, each
one, the island round moon gate
famous for honeymooners to pose in.

The circular floral design,
a Maypole of England's gardens
washed by rain and the U.K.'s timid sun,

a soft soap for fair skin. Mimic
the embroidery hoops which tidied
women's hands in Victorian Times.

My kitchen closet full of the plus,
minuses of time, a handle to
a Minton soup tureen gone missing,

like an ear shot off in battle. The
set linen dinner tablecloth, a Julian
Schnabel canvas of cracked plates.

As if a Lascaux bull roared
through my dark cave of eatery
wares. Smashed ceramics forged

from crushed ancestral bones,
the ones ground up, and daintily
painted, to make such wildness tame.

Jigsaw

Like pieces of a jigsaw puzzle,
reefs around the island, a part

of the whole on the tablecloth
of the Atlantic. I sit on the beach,

each wave crested forms into
the White Cliffs of Dover, origins

of the island culture when ship
wrecked ancestors landed from

a boat bashed apart like a native paw
paw, scattered seeds from which I grew.

Sea salted with an inner rhythm
perpetually rocked by the undertow,

the low pitch sound of a pull back
tide down into the celestial deep.

Angelfish flashed light like stars where I
moon walked the sands below, buoyant.

My Pink Computer

Words need a body, the flesh
to be born, the pink tongued
mouth of mothering. Words

need the earth, the pink
sand I first scrawled with
a stick, the tiny crushed

mollusks full of the sea's
memory. Words need
a heart, the pumped line

of veins with the beat, beat
of sound first heard in a sonic
womb. Words need skin.

Pink Wall Clock

Like island time it slows
down, as if a pie where
the knife gets stuck
in the Suriname cherry filling,

the hand becomes weighted,
wobbly. The numbers, years
marked in icing on a child's
birthday cake. Hours passing,

flamingo stick figure legs
stride. The Empire sun sets,
all magenta skies and lacy clouds,
a strawberries and cream dessert.

Inner Tube

The bright pink inner tube
a belly button I float in
age three, forever mothered
by the sea, rocking me
as if in a cradle. Waves

flow over me, stretch into
frilly tide like dresses I try on,
take off in a summer's day
of sea salt smells and heat.
The practiced thrill of

letting go of the soft sand
floor, leaping from toes
on point, to fly adrift the gulf
stream turquoise blue
with my nest underarms.

Sun Spots

The shredded light my straw
hat shed was like grains of
wheat falling on my shoulders

from the crown's stout silo.
I was a fruit ripening in
semitropical heat. Now spots,

like seeds inside, implode,
grow their own geography,
a chain of Caribbean islands

surface, link over my chest,
tattoo for the sun's expeditions.
One, the size of a shilling, blood

money spent for a golden tan,
the regal feel of its glow, the silky
sensation, summer is my skin.

Sun Prayers

The images of the deceased African
Bermudians in the Royal Gazette
were heartwarming to me. Photo

complete with bio underneath,
like cricket trading cards in death's
ultimate out of the Somerset Stadium

game. Badges to get on the *People
get ready, there is a train
a coming!* for the above the ground

railroad trail. I want their faith
when I die. I want the dialect tones
of their voices, soft sun prayers

of sea wave sounds and lightning
strikes weather cutting the landscape
in two. Brimming with a habitation's

sea-weedy shores and habits. Lazy
moments when a tongue curls in heat,
a flame in a sermon's slow fire. About

the home of oleander maiden hills,
the marshy toad land, the fossilized
limestone earth where a body will

finally lie. Curved rib bones, like
scaffolding of the ships that brought
us here. I want these saints present.

House of Mirrors

The slap, slap of the wave
against sand, sound of
a woman kneading pastry,
the tide rimmed as a crust.

The underwater house of
mirrors, torsos swell into
Willendorf Venuses and
a jelly fish floats adrift like

an auntie's church hanky.
The urge to float constant,
remain aloft before the wave
throws an arm over

my shoulder to enlist me,
spins my body around
a turbulent wringer in deep
wash currents. Tiny mollusks

litter my footprints as I
come out of the tide like
false toe nails I shed as I
regain my land locked stride.

I have sand in my hair,
Papier-Mache strands,
stiffening locks like a Jester's
hat, I have had to adorn.

Bermuda Blue

I say to Greg, my computer man,
it is grey not blue, as he takes my new
laptop out of the Dell box which says
blue in its description. But it is
the deep navy blue of tunics I wore
at Bermuda High School for Girls,

as if dyed in the Parker Ink we wrote
our lessons in,' Purity and Strength'
the school motto. Something immaculate
about how the letter blocks are laid
out, school desks face a blackboard
in obedience. But a shrill randomly

emits from this machine, the sound
of the island frogs' whistling. Calls
me back to the oleander scent,
the loquat tree's fruit dropping,
the surf's constant rehearsing for
the large seventh wave, the day's heat

caught in the smell of the ocean. And I
remember how to write, tell the island's
story on an instrument starched to the perfection
of nautical edges. The latitude, longitude
of precise writing. Take my uniform off,
go for a swim, leap from a ship shape craft.

Feed Bag

Why at age seventy, I start
to use an Island Shop bag
with a Bermuda house and
Long Tails embroidered
on it? Canvas with handles,

the snaffles from which
a feed bag hangs, say on
carriage horses on Front Street.
Remember? I do, I stroked
manes, hand, a small monkey

on their backs, they tried to
shake off. Pink, yellow punctuate
the scene similar to an Azorean
handkerchief I carried. I think
of the loops of thread in the air,

momentary wings, the tying
of the scene down, the knot left,
splayed like an anchor. The needle
going through, the minute holes
creating the precision of pointillism

built with tiny stitches. I thread
my hand through the round
handles' eye, lodge it in my elbow's
crook, hold a medallion of mirth,
like a talisman close to my body.

Long Tale

The kiskadee, with a yellow
waist coat, is full of himself.
White streaks on face
the stuff of action heroes.

The bolts of electricity
as if heat shocked from
flying too close to the sun.
The robins in their burlap

rags, hop, hop, to the day's
crumbs, like I did in sack
races at BHS. I mimic
the Longtail, burrow myself

in a room on cliffs above
the greeting sea, in the Long
Tale of my returning, leaving
each year at summer's end.

Ironing

I wriggle the iron like Rita
taught me as I press the linen
shirt. A tadpole floats
up the waves of blue.

I press the steam button,
it exhales like a horse
after a race, sweaty and
proud. No matter how

I try, I cannot un-wrinkle
the whole fabric, each corner
a too tight shoe in which
the steel toe can't fit. I

smooth out your collar,
cuffs, the stocks for your
neck, hands, so when in
public you are presentable.

Winter Survival

Let the bright white light
cascading through your home
in search of colour, show you,
you always wanted to paint
your sorry trashcans battered
silver grey from a long war

of use, the colour of a mango.
When you spray the liquid, you
become a hibiscus blooming a petal.
When you hold up the orange tin
can top, it is a shield against the cold.
And then when you must also colour

the condiment shelves yellow, it
is like the island sun reviving
your own senses. The island must
always be near. More so in the snow,
heaped like a rolled up canvas against
your home's edge which invites filling.

Immense and Clumsy

Elephant like, steel grey body,
immense and clumsy on
our driveway, the Waterworks

truck ambles up, brings water
through a hose like a rubbery trunk,
to thwart the threat of extinction.

Greystones' whitewashed roof
like snow melting provides daily
needs from caught tropical rain.

A silver bullet tank shoots down
Lover's Lane, the perfect weapon
for a season of drought when

a wild herd of cumulous elude,
roam, until lightning whips them
back into the island's bone-thin hand.

From Afar

Via google world map,
Bermuda's white washed
roofs look like tropic birds
landed on a small island
to rest before they fly on.

Closer in, like Chiclets
poured out of a packet,
each a remaining frontal tooth
bites into the land, chews it up.
From the plane flying

in the evening, the light
softens their angular pitch,
and it looks more like
the sea's white tips have
claimed it, taken it back under.

Tidely

The scat outside my kitchen door, like mounds
of sargassum on Grape Bay, flies, shape,
equal. There, like a bear, jaws of the sea
open in each guttural wave, as the rising
surf relentlessly paws the land. Here,

a body to body fight with a beast, scary. There,
the ocean although vast, more likely to change
its mind, leave me facedown, a scanned
document imprinted in sand, like memory
works something until lodged, then rushes to

prowl new ground. The retelling of family
lost aboard ships, like water rushing, receding,
makes a death soothing, a lullaby in
the history of whom the Atlantic devoured,
then left the remains, so washed over, tidily behind.

Hurricane Humberto

The video I watch shows casuarinas fidgety
around houses, branches lively as baby
fingers above a pram as the wind bawls.

A friend tells me the earth is trying to get
rid of us. Here, an uprooted mangrove tree
is the storm's wishbone, keen to eliminate

occupants. One roof is wrapped in plastic,
like an islander might wind around
the head in a squall, turquoise as a surgical

cap after chemotherapy. In the bright
sunshine and quiet, after Hurricane Humberto
has gone back out to sea, left the island

with palms bent over, converts to a
ruthless doctrine, the white washed
roofs line up into paper soldier hats.

Island Wave

The taxi driver beeps the horn,
raises his forefinger above
the steering wheel: the Bermuda wave.

Like the island's Skink lizard,
peering above a banana leaf,
just enough effort. On old British

racing green Morris Minors,
the traffic signals would open
on each side, like the dewlap

the anole displays for mating and
to be territorial. The National
Geographic article says they change

skin for camouflage when in
new terrain, like the sun's patterns of
shadow and light on the car's roof, conceal

passengers in its daily hide and seek
game, although each a.m. its fiery long
digits hail, hail at us from the earth's edge.

Cousins I Never Met

for Wendy Frith

The lad is lying on the couch
in CBC's Games Room, watches
the Muppets on the screen,
large as a sail that pulls his
canvas mat like a craft to sea.

I'm at the computer where keys
rattle, the loose teeth in an old
person's mouth. I can't figure out
on such a dated machine
how to email an island relative.

I hear a young English voice say:
Madam may I help you? And
like a gambler throws dice,
his hand scurries over the boxed
numbers, instantly opens the digital

highway. I later learn the two are
my cousins, grans of the cousin I
email. How connected we are on
such a small island, already entwined
before we are gathered up by the net.

Cricket Match

Outside my window, my Adirondack chair, all white
and striped by the sun with cutting edges, is a Cricket
goal keeper crouching. Memories take me back to the isle.

I watch Live Stream Cup Match on my p.c. The close up
of a batter, a pearl in the luminous clam shell of my laptop
connection. The bat is an oar from a punt in Sinky Bay,

used to row to a larger vessel. The batter holds it up to break
the wave of the pitch crashing into it. Men dressed in white,
suitable for a moon walk, so delicate to keep the balance

within the spin of a curving ball. The padding appropriate for
biological warfare. To some spectators, enemy's tactics unseen,
rules refined, hidden. In August the island divides into sides.

St Georges for where the Sea Venture landed, and Somerset
for 'God's country' parish. The island so entwined, opponents
come from the same source. Both names match the founder.

Good Friday Kite

We pasted pink, yellow, orange
tissue triangles together to take

the bright craft upwards unlike
our history of ships downed

by one. Made of the kaleidoscope
patterns, I would see when I held

one to my eye, a sea captain
looking through a telescope for

lands unknown. The South Shore on
a Good Friday is a sky of handmade

kites with tails, like shooting stars.
Multi-prism window, with an escape

rope of tied sheets, less it flies
too close to the sun and burns.

If This

If this is the sea breathing,
then it is nasal,
deep, congested,
and it often clears its throat.

If this is the palm arcing,
then it is feathery,
a fledgling bird poised,
about to take off.

If these are clouds forming,
they are indecisive,
bunches of paper
about to be tossed.

If this is the day starting,
amongst the cumulus
marble chips, filling up
the blue's fresh vacancy.

If this is the sun rising,
a coin pressed from the horizon's
burning line, metallic, sharp
with brisk steam rising.

If this is me without you,
house so empty before I
left, then let me return there
with the boldness of beginnings.

Secret Society

Straw

Like the straw that broke
the camel's back, wispy plastic
ones could clog an ecosystem.

The pink striped twirl, a merry go
round post, we have ridden
in circles for ages, like the up

down movement of waves, as
we floated above a semitropical
glassy sea floor. Impervious to

the sun's gold ring we reached
for in holiday days. Like the suck
of a waterspout over South Shore

comes in close, disturbs. Overheated,
we have sipped away the ocean,
in gulps, almost swallowed it whole.

The Queen is Here

In Washington D.C. on
a stately visit, where a motorcade
sounds like dogs on a hunt
yelping at their dead prey,
and the police cars
megaphone light from roofs.

At the launch of a ship in
Bristol, where a slide like
a grinding tool sharpens
the keel as it lowers into sea.
Cuts the empire's path into
the globe's round plenty.

Under the palace chandelier,
where a multi-handed Durga
wages the war of cheery light
in history's dark gloom, hangs
above the royal carpet of blood,
flowed to pink stain the world.

Nest

The nest the robin built
so low above my front
door could be a garden
party hat Princess Beatrice
or Eugenia wears to a wedding,
Royal Punk Posh. Or a basket

a Kenyan might carry on
her head for days, balances
a cargo of fresh eggs to get to
the Nairobi market. A patch
of pubic hair I am pushed
out from under each a.m.

between legs of sturdy portal
frames. But I want this poem
to move up, not have a down-
ward motion. The mother bird
zooms a line, beak, a needle,
threads air, pulls the hem of

the sky just so, to make shells
turn fragile blue. And when
an empty one falls, the cracked
shape is all British pram with
a bonnet, from whence a small
embryo sun was cradled, rose.

Purity and Strength

The purity of centuries of
pristine breeding rolls out
the red carpet of blood.

The strength of taking
a beloved horse over a jump,
the many obstacles before her.

The serene look of sitting in
a Faberge Easter Egg carriage,
without knowing what will hatch.

The Queen's face upon every
notebook at BHS above its motto:
'purity and strength.' Oval as

a medallion, tiara saint for me to
aspire to in all lessons. Your
portrait at the Bermuda airport

is one when you are young,
you turn to the left, not at your
subjects, avoid the Royal Gaze.

The view requires a side glance,
the royal crown on your forehead
holds diamonds sharp as horns.

Aeronautics

The hot air balloon
hangs an exclamation mark
in the Victorian sky! All

the boasts of empire needs
to rise, get a view, if from
a large rambling British picnic basket.

Sights galore, if not unsettling,
the expanse of stars, a world
un-mapped by any conqueror,

beyond where a sun rises,
sets, blushing the world, if
only to return to earth, deflated.

The Sun's Sorrow

Like a lineup of sunflowers,
the standing lamps I will
take to the dump hang
heavy heads, worn out from duty.

The bulbs, GE, come in cardboard
boxes, like Bosch Pears, golden,
skin, full of juicy white meat,
make any table glow with goodness.

Each shaped like a teardrop, as
if the sun's sorrow is evident
within them for not being
able to brighten the whole world.

Elgin

History has just driven down
Nettleton Hollow. The machine
repairing the road has 'Elgin'
written on it. I think of the white

muscled statues, like the strength
of a civilization Britain stole,
transported as it made itineraries
into the world. I think of the word

Elgin, and how it has slowly
travelled like the snail shaped
vehicle moving past my home.
A chip of stone, blocky, on

the road's shoulder. Words,
ransacked, taken from an original
site, attach to new meanings as
we route out our thoughts, domains.

Accordion

A bookshelf with two bookends,
each note has its own story,
the accordion player squeezes,

like a dried flower flattened
under a stack of texts. A large
Black Bible a preacher hauls,

maneuvers. Bellows, a snake
he tames, a shuffle of cards
he deals to tell your life's truth.

Dove

The brand name evokes peace,
soft, gentle, the flight of escape,
the cooing of feeling safe and clean.

Why not that it means *dove,* as in
off a high cliff into waters, surfy
as soap lathers on a body. The going

down deep. Maybe it isn't a feathery
calm a girl wants at the end of the day,
with the line of suds on her torso forming

wings that flap into a settling. Rather,
the tide line of a rocky shore she survived,
came out of, dripping a foamy sea, and dirt free!

Tea Kettle

A Viking's helmet
is atop my stove,
the glare of the enemy
reflects in the stainless
steel, everything un-hot

in my kitchen. The lever
to the top like a wing.
Steams, like warriors
out of breath trapesing
over a mountain to fight.

The brew I make from
it is the tawny colour of
ruin from all the battles
fought for it. Helmets
have been used to boil

water on a fire through
the ages. Soldiers huddled
want a taste of home as
the world blows up around
them, and bullets whistle

by like a tea kettle's sound.
I pick it up like an iron
releasing heat, evening out
the transparent air as I too want
calm in the day's skirmishes.

Silver Toast Rack

Even toast must be neatened,
like folded laundry, placed in an
order to be crisp, like a collar,
not soggy as from British rain.

Shirts hung from hangers, each
filed into space to dry. Curvaceous
frame, ribs of a roast. The best part
of Sunday dinner, a slice mops

up gravy as if a porous hanky.
A group of jumps for the well
placed mare, the lineup for a race
at Ascot. Brown bodies tower

above each gate. How to have
bread cool, not become a heap,
sluggish, remain a platform, to
firmly butter, to ensure it is a task.

Every cloud has a silver lining,
like when white envelopes are placed
in gleaming rungs on a desk, the daily
manna of paying bills, arranged.

Auerbach Shows Up

In the roof of my 'Semitropical
Paint Hut' paintings, his stroke
like a T.V antennae sticking out.

Years walking London to view
his 'Primrose Hill.' The lobotomy
experiments of Bacon's portraits,

and Freud's nudes served like
a thin slab of breakfast pork.
The rimmed light in the fat.

Nothing terribly British about
them, rather postwar gloom,
in a city shredded as a destroyed

canvas, ripped from stretchers
like a Phyllida Barlow sculpture.
To try to finish a painting is to

ruin its chances, rather to be thrown
from its wave when it touches shore.
Balance atop currents. I learned

colour on an island where Jacaranda
hung dragon's teeth rich with
blood, yellow was boasted from

a kiskadee breast, and blues
wavered with the sea's darks, lights,
a hallucinated sixties tie dye shirt.

Secret Society

My Bermudian cousin says
make sure the windows have
locks, as if they keep the outside
view of hibiscus, frangipani secure.

I press the rental cottage's digital code
to let myself in, feel I have
become a member of a secret society.
On Front Street in Hamilton, I hold

my leather tote bag close to my chest
like a shield, remove gold jewelry
as I did as a child before I swam,
so as not to attract the Barracuda.

Become sensitive to my tropical
surroundings as Cephalopods
receiving light waves through
turquoise waters in Harrington Sound.

I've come here to Paget to write,
pull down shades if at night,
hide the computer's glow like
practices used in a WWII Black Out.

When my mother read mail at the
British Navy Quarters. Deciphered
a hidden code by what was left out,
much like island tourist brochures.

Flight from Egypt

Something must be slain.
The brown poisonous skin peeled, so
white meat emerges as a purity, as

layers bow over to the process, when
a blade frees. Nature guards its
treasures. A multi fingered vegetable,

like an African diaspora of countries
dependent on a hardy crop in
unnourished soils. Mimics the flight

from Egypt, modest beginnings
are made princely. A golden
batter of eggs, sugar, butter

adorns the cassava's flavours.
Like a large British saddle bag
opens, full of a Caribbean journey.

Heritage Parade 2019

No one is dressed appropriately,
except the elder African Bermudian
women with straw hats neatening
the sun's light with the braiding
coiled like a lasso. Paper fans open,
close, a book on proper etiquette,

white gloves in laps, lilies. Soldiers
deftly wield drumsticks as if eating
carefully off the white plate of
a Royal Regiment Drum. Pith helmet,
a souffle peak strapped down. Long
uniform stripes on trousers, loop

tassels on jackets, like each footman is
a sleek whistle for the Queen's Empire.
Gombey headdress tapers up into peacock
feathers, the pride of tribal history.
A dancer plays a game of leaping hide
and seek, camouflaged in case of danger.

Portuguese women in long cotton skirts,
scarves covering hair, nuns on the way
to prayer, mimic scattering seed in a field
as they march, like dispersing holy water.
A farmhand carries a large axe on his back,
cross for the stubbled route of daily work.

Spectators legs in the black hole of Spanx,
shrinks a body to a core. The Goddess Nike's
wing stitched by shoestrings on each foot
like a wound closing. The African Bermudian
majorette, maidenhead of the parade, twirls
batons in each hand, propellers to lift her off.

It is Good Friday

It is Good Friday and I'm not pulling
a tissue coloured kite in from the ocean
breeze, like downing a star. It is Good

Friday and I'm not going to church at
3 p.m. to observe Christ's body mapped
on the latitude, longitude of pain. It is

Good Friday and I'm listening to the hollow
climb out of winter, see buds appear,
a congregation speaks in tongues. It is

Good Friday and I'm writing a poem,
a death in itself, to harness one's own
experience to words, shut it up in a tomb.

So Right

Something so right about
the American flag draped
on the door of an old colonial.

The same simple lines speak of
beginnings. Hung vertically,
the rocket's fuel trail of going

to the moon, the unknown of
new territory. In a country where
people always reach for the stars

to become one. Houses with stone
hearths full of ashes, as if one fell,
shooting down the chimney's

dark hole. Fallen from the sky's
banner, combusts, so a human can
hold palms to it just for warmth.

Smoke

What exactly did she scribble
on the air with the white chalk of
her cigarette butt, now lying in black
ashes, like from a cremated body.

A curved question mark rises,
all fuzzy in its query? Words
blown apart, the un-said apparition
of an un-formed language. What

exactly was she taking in when
she sucked from its tip like
a straw sugar cane candy? And
why the need to see that she,

in fact, breathes, the funneled
drama of fumes, coming from her,
like a fury. The rings she forms
with her lips, a fish's mouth

groping. Life preserves, she
throws out in the tide of waves.
What fire does she put out when
she grinds the flame into the dish,

a bright finger nail clawing?
What path, do the inches of each
stub mark? Linked through years
of her outrunning the ghost of smoke.

Polar

The Russian poet says in Paris she feels like
an iceless polar bear. One drifts on a flow, piece

of the Artic jigsaw puzzle, a beach surfer riding
a board. A fan coral in Anguilla is bleached snow

white as the Gulf streams tepid water. Rabbitfish,
brushstrokes in a watery sky, as they run to Canada.

White Out

A friend has early dementia,
sentences resemble WWII
deciphered mail. Spaces
in her speech like white out

was used. I remember in Italy
when I used my tourist
Italian, words seemed to race
around the one I plopped

down in the middle of a
phrase, like a travel satchel
in a train station near the tracks.
Plunked down near motorists in

an Italian rotary. As we age
our brain connects slowly. It
took twentyfour hours to
remember Sally Mann's name

after a conversation on photography.
When I did recall it, I was like
a shepherd welcoming home
a lost sheep into the flock.

Parting

And so my hair resumes a natural
part, left sided. Unlike the middle road
I made it into in the sixties when a woman
aimed to part one when she walked. Braids

on each side, reins hanging. A horse's
head free of a rider, about to take off,
horizons so near. What does this return
me to? The right eye, in danger of being

unseen, an ancestor privateer's patch. Once
it was flirtatious to draw a strand back when
mystery was the desire. Now, a plastic brush
holds follicles of a past, in its claw, knotted.

My locks wiry as I age, a Viking helmet
of silver from fierce growth, a Brillo pad
scours all unwanted thoughts. Curls flow
a currency of electrical wires blown white hot.

Green Space

The Pakistani says the villagers
don't want him to grow
fruit trees on the green,
with a tendency to drop
bright cargo, purses spilling seed,
old world coinage onto the earth.

Want morning glories, asters
instead, like embroidery
everywhere, nothing to do but
cling to fences, soften the green air.
Little megaphones filled with
the whispering hush of rain.

But his village had orchards,
offered what might sweeten a meal,
or when regimes shuffled, to crush
what joy they found. Persimmons
stored ovules, prayer beads the earth
rotates for a future, if they had to flee.

Man on the Moon

The U.S. was not the first to try,
Egyptians aligned pyramids so
a pharaoh might lift off straight
into heaven. We know we come

from stars, when a shooting one
curves in the dark, like a celestial
Adam's rib we connect to a part
of ourselves. Its geometric curve,

a rainbow, we remember. A man
on the moon is so different than
a woman. She is one, we know.
But a man had to go there, connect

to a cyclical self than bounce on
it like a kid on a bed. Stand inside
his own speech bubble, peer out
of its fish bowl, have nothing to say.

The Old Schoolhouse

I can imagine the hand that pulled the bell rope
down to begin the day, then released it, palm
flying up into the air like a bird seeking sky.

I can imagine the hand of the child raising an arm
like a shoot in a garden, fingers wanting to reach
for new knowledge and how it held the world.

I can imagine the hand that held the rag that
scrubbed the blackboard of today's lessons
so that tomorrow's might gather its rows

of letters, toy soldiers march forward to fight
ignorance. I can't imagine the hand that put
a four-sided window in the cupola, an ice cube

even summer's lightning won't melt. Nor the hand
that neatened the sideboards which had eased
into themselves, with straight lines as if drawn

by a ruler. Neither the one which replaced the door
latch's compass arc for a knob. A nail sticking out,
banged in hard to keep a portal shut. I can't imagine

the hand that removed the bell rocking its pendulum
back forth, like a cat's tail clock. Nor can I imagine,
who made the spire point up into a sharp dunce cap?

Bell

The Bell of his name rings everywhere
in I phones, rotaries, the ones that detach
from walls, curve in the hand like small pets.

Today, I await the dial tone sound, wait
for it to fall, a liquid drop, down into
the ripple of my ear, like the heroine in

Jewel in the Crown, awakens at night to
the torrents' *hushing!* Signal the rains
had finally come. Such silence today, even

for one without TV, cell, lives by herself,
lest I think my psyche not programmed by
the trifling of connection, like an ancestor

in Devon waited for the toll that called
a village to assemble. A megaphone blaring
because some hand pulled a rope in urgency,

tugged on the heavens' mouth in the apex
of a town tower to solicit a conversation,
be heard. The rope and bell at Christ Church,

a navel string from the Caribbean islands
buried in me, planted like a flower when
I was in the boom box of my Bermudian

mother's womb, heard the peal, peeling
of her heart, in the circle of sonic sound,
that told in its spasms, washing over me

like the surfside sea of South Shore,
rolling around my body, constantly
chorusing a chant that I was not alone.

Garden of Eden

Eyes hang like fruit off
the brows' branches.

Nose, the tree trunk
down, nostrils flare out

rooted by nasal hairs.
Lips, snake wriggling.

Leonora's Landscape

A relief to know the Mexicans talk to the dead,
so many ghosts in Europe after the wars. Here, I feel
I am in one of my landscapes, Muertos face paintings,
green cacti, burro taxis, seen in one glance. I was told Surrealism
was born because of the camera. The lens' winking eye
fooled the world. I think after two World Wars, one
goes crazy, stretches figures across a canvas like a torture rack.

In the market today peasants beat a pinata, like my prayers
pelted God in Spain when I was insane, demanded treats after
Max's arrest. Here, roadside altars to Mary abound, replicate
kiosks in my English village, Madonna called on for the day's
errands. Cuernavaca pilgrims balance skulls on sticks, like balls
in a circus, play with the deceased. I remember tombstones in
the family cemetery at Clayton, shields we propped up against
death.

Dreaming

Of course, Van Gogh is in the room
with these late summer sunflowers,
the twisted trees of Arles, like hands
wringing with tension. And, oh,
that burst of stars, for a final
letting go. All the yellow of the fields
with their combed rows, now above,
hanging, fireflies one could swirl
a stick through, paint spattered on
heavens' cloth as Yeats called dreaming.

Love Songs

You know when you see someone
on stage with a guitar that they
will sing mostly love songs.

Will try while crooning not to
play wrong notes, have fingers
trip up on the chords, a lover's

legs walking the tight rope path.
Will stop mid song to tune
the tone, tighten the pegs,

like holding an ex by the ear. And
you in the audience will stare through
strings into the instrument's sound hole,

remember how the moon rose one
night, just so, above the ocean's waves.
Notice the guitar is so tenderly

held, like a worn stuffed animal,
now without ligaments or features,
taken into one's dreamy sleep.

Latitude, Longitude

Thaw

The patches of snow in
the field, jagged, scattered,
disheveled bedsheets,

someone had a fitful night
of sleep. Thaw brings fever,
furor, and a twitch of discontent.

The Cream of Wheat I pour
is sleet, is snow, slushes into
my breakfast cereal. Kernels,

once the braided light of
a Midwestern farm girl's hair,
swayed adoration to the sun,

in yellow's summer swoon.
The house wants winter's
pleated ice-boned corset off.

Sounds of water drip, dripping
from the gutter on the porch,
the *splat! splat!* of spitting.

Days at Sea

The front porch icicles hang, winter's icy teats.
What is comfort in the cold, but memories

of ancestral sea captains sailing in solitude
out in the ocean? Here the hills tuck

barren trees into their pitched curve
like the masts of vessels going down.

The fire raises its own bright sail above
the log, drawn up strands meet, two hands

clap for warmth. Days at sea, days at home,
aloneness one's guest. 12x12 panes, welcome

barricades, the boiler's booming sound,
stacks of a ship blaring as it comes into port.

Latitude, Longitude.

The downpour from the faucet
steely, a sewing machine's needle
stitches the rumpled cloth of liquid
below. My knees rise from

the flat water surface, mountains
from a lake. Where am I when
I begin a morning bath?
After the shower's veil

has adorned my head,
made me bridal before
I make the day's vows. Do
I float in my white tub

like Moses in a basket
to a new kingdom?
And where exactly do
my wet foot prints go,

before they dry on the tiles'
squares? Like the blocks
of a nautical map, finding
my hurried latitude, longitude.

Not Exactly

While not exactly milking a cow,
there are similarities. I attend the flow

of the leaking copper pipes. The arc
of the water sprouts, like a wing evolved

from years tunneling underground. I think
of women who walk miles through a desert

to get one pan full of water for a family,
and shut my mouth. Old houses, old bones,

like an ancestor's ship with a hole in its side,
I keep watch, time the dripping down of

drops, like sand grains in an hour glass.
The plumbers want me to replace copper

with plastic pipes. A hip replacement
of sorts, like when friends boast new ligaments,

as if FAO Schwartz Toys gone to the Doll
Hospital to mend. I have loved to think

of the golden means of water cursing
through a bright maze beneath my home,

the balance of excess and deficiency,
like an English Garden of spouting magnolia

topiaries, and hibiscus hedges with butch haircuts.
Here a kitchen faucet turned on is a lily blooming.

Re-Fresh

The winter landscape, leathery
as an elephant's hide, holds the years
memories in a luminous creased bag.

My tracks indent the glassy surface,
I am weighed down too, a slow beast,
carry the past. I shovel into it,

activate its glare, throw snow
over my shoulders as if to refresh
my backside with a trunk of water.

Christmas Landscape

Red Christmas bows turn lamppost,
house, dog into festive presents.
Waves of green on fences fall,
rise in peaks to wreaths like life
preservers. Bob in an ocean, as we
ride the tides of the season, try to

stay afloat. We collect branches
in urns: fresh, fragrant, verdant,
as the landscape becomes marbled
by the lined ruins of bare trees.
Cards arrive in the mail, open
flap, the peaked roof of a church,

brings messaged praise. Even
the robust snowman has been
given a scarf, jacket, boots,
gloves to wear before he,
like the homeless, disappears
into winter's clean up act.

Post Christmas

I cut the branches from
the un-decorated tree,
shortened limbs make it
a hat rack for passing Advent
visitors. I hold up two pieces
by the bark, spread fans to heed
the fire's flow. They crackle
like a blown electrical fuse,

fill the room with the smell
of incense. Smoke flaps
its amorphous wing, rises
to heaven where stars button
up the dark. I sit in this cave
of light, hear logs move
as they burn, like oxen
shifting haunches in a stable.

The Afterlife of Christmas Trees

No longer like rockets about to ascend,
supercharging homes with brightness, merriment,
they stand at windows, unlit, like carousels turned

off. Lights no longer guiding one round and
round into a spin, the twirl of a season's spirits
up, down. Now a present emerges which won't

fit under a tree, but needs all the boxes of
a calendar where the owner stuffs them full,
then ticks off each with a tidy bow. Now

trees stand quietly, still dressed, look out,
water flower-ish, avoiding a dance, seek
the time before they were swept off their feet.

CROSSED

Like i's dotted, the lit Advent
candles in windows become
birthday lights for the New Year.

A time when individuals do
such, cross t's, look forward
to the Easter one. After winter's

sleet, like bent sails pull towards
a center, a pilgrim is marked with
a latitude, longitude drawn in ashes.

Sea-Through

The Garden Center employee
Nick, throws the tree onto my Jag,
and ties it through opened
windows, tightens twine like the girth

of a saddle. This tree will transport
me into the holiday season. It is a rocket
ready to launch from my moving vehicle.
It miraculously stands up straight and tall

at seven feet, like a metronome centering. I
adorn it with island pink, turquoise balls,
much seen in seafood huts on the coast, often
enmeshed in fish nets. Where wind chimes

made from thin shells hang from doors
like a sole earring on a privateer. How we
bring our home with us wherever we are,
like Christ brought heaven to earth. I use

to swim underwater in the harbour, hear
boats bobbing, buoys teeming, sounds
like gears changing in a large rusty machine,
the sea, the mechanics, the force in my universe.

Squirrel Fish

The large town maintenance
truck, red as a squirrel fish,
drips snow from its shovel
like from a lower lip, to stripe

its steel belly with white. Headlights
shine their lines down the road,
measure the height of snow in
inches like a tide tables chart I read

on my island. And like the squirrel,
which jumps in a trapeze artist way,
tempts a no net existence, I leap
too, gather metaphors, like nuts in

a tree's trunk, store words inside.
To feed on, so I can live in this
blank page, shape sentences
on a luminous tablet. The fire red,

as a nocturnal squirrel fish feeding,
flames fin the logs as it becomes one,
devours facts, so I can write this
poem to stay warm, survive winter.

Would Be

Big, blustering, bragging, would be blizzard,
trees covered in snow, blank speech blurbs,
white hot air balloons, try to make peace.

Kitchen mixer spinners drip icing, white
souffle eggs. Blown light bulbs, crackling
pieces of glass everywhere. Mattress springs

bursting through, entwined ripped sheets
above the deadbeat flat bed of earth. Bush,
the whiskery, veined inside of a dog's ear.

Ermine

Like the trees have thrown off ermine
mink stoles, clumps of snow line
the driveway on my way back from

the postbox. Steely, it disappears in a winter
storm, red flag an emergency signal, small
hatchet breaks apart the cold. I go out to

retrieve it as winds knock it off the post. Ice
chips on its door, pebbles on a tongue in a Greek
orator's mouth, practices annunciating spring.

Sermon

The snowdrops hold petals above
the earth in a deep freeze moment,
snow drops will no longer fall.

Like birds opening beaks
to be fed, snowdrops lift
up to the sun's warmth.

Slices of ice around stone walls,
like cleric collars taken off after
winter's long sermon. Last night's

rainstorm flashed light around
the house, a police car on an emergency
call, searching the hills for spring.

Housekeeper

My cousin asks,"Do you have a housekeeper?"
Yes, if I count the Domestic House spider
which collects flies in its net like fallen trapeze

artists. Yes, if I count the winter mouse crawling
out of the kitchen corner in a grey monk's garb,
hungry for daily bread, tail like a whip

to flagellate itself. Yes, if I count
the hammerhead vacuum eating debris like
sargassum wedged between the wavy-sea grains

of chestnut. Yes, if I count the robins whose nest
of chicks above the house portal is full of bright
song, a doorbell rung announcing spring's arrival.

Seal

I spray the screen door,
long tendrils of water spout
out of a head, a large summer
spider scrambles a screen.

Above is the robin's nest,
wedged like a wax seal
on a note mid eighteenth
century. What message do

they bring each year? After
they make a home for chicks,
and then leave it empty, mud

ridden, stuck, like a piece
of used up gum. What bangs
open, shut, like a flapping
wing as I exit and enter?

Un Tidy

The maple yellow ringed,
as leaves begin to brighten
at tips of branches, a halo
for having stood still
through winter's long calm.

The forsythia lines of yellow,
the curved light of rainbows,
wispy thrusts, thrashing
to be born, the untidy
golden hair of an infant.

The bridge of courage we
need to come up out of winter,
each bud on the lighted
path to show the way, moving
through, exiting a tunnel.

The Poem is Here

Where the geranium leaves yellow
into a coward's colour as I have made
them one from over watering, dependent.

In the thin frail trail of clouds above
the lake's beach, as if the back bone of
the sky is withered by such balmy heat.

The poem is here where the side mirrors
on my Jag flash light like dueling swords
for the road's trail ahead. And the sun

rolls around in the opening in the roof,
like a ball in a box, bouncing from
the thrust of speed, unable to remain in borders.

The Poem is Here

Where the yellow raft is a slab
of butter melting on the hot grey
griddle of the shiny lake.

Where the boat's prow lifts
water on its sides like wings,
a bird trying to take off, fly. Here

where yesterdays' daylilies
droop, tongue-tied from
speaking too loudly about the sun.

In the hose's circles, like a rope
to ring the bell of the showerhead,
scattering notes on the geranium.

The Poem is Here

Where the American flags
on the way into town are
tongues, red streaked from
licking the sun. Box of stars,
glittering ice to cool a throat down.

The Poem is Here,

Where the anole lizard
unfolds an orange dewlap
half mooned on his throat,
like a cd disk fed into a player.

Here where the surf throws
itself over the rocks, like white
clothe over furniture when a grand
house is closed for the season.

Here where two swimmers,
like Ken and Barbie dolls,
are being wrapped by the turning
plastic sea through waters. Here

where summer rain shimmers heat
with the back light of the sun. Angel
wings descend the white washed roof
with slippers into the tank's shoebox.

So Familiar

Doug is sitting in his tractor,
relaxed as someone watching
T.V. as he peers through the wide
glass view of his cabin. I imagine

he is almost dozing, the hypnotic flow
of grass bending in waves as his
John Deere comb parts the field's hair.
His vehicle like a postal truck, throws

mail to the sides. He turns the meadow
into an open book, and my summer
in Washington, CT begins with this
sound, familiar as a husband snoring.

Humidity

Daylily petals curl, limber back,
like a banana peeled, split open,
dead headed buds, soft as small
island plantains I would eat.

How the humidity takes me back
to summer days there when
a tee shirt would stick to
a gardener's torso like wrinkled

skin of a mango. Waves rising
on South Shore majestic,
threatened with a peaked power,
quick as a python striking. One

learned to dive into, like tackling
an opponent in sport as it topples
over one's back, rushes towards
a goal. Hard to have one in

this heat, when a breeze barely
moves through the bottom
of a cracked window, welcome
as a lover's note slipped under a door.

Canned Summer

The rolls of hay lie on their sides,
as if summer has been canned,
put in tins for the duration of winter.

I see the farmer driving them down
Nettleton Hollow, carpets rolled up
to create a wider space. A round of beef,

the girth of the fatted calf, the cycle
present when covered in white
plastic, make them protrude like molars.

Postures

The lone Geranium in the Mexican glass,
stem thin and firm, a plume in ink. What
would a flower write? Tell me? Its cluster

of buds, butterflies. Ascend from the wriggling
life of worms, intimate with soil. Slants in the angle
of an ostrich with feathers backed up to the sky

while head remains in sand. All postures I take
to make words fly. A flower known to bear heat,
parched days, thrives in spite of lack of rain. I

water one, liquid bows over in a stream before
entering roots, the map of fingers holding mud as I too,
clutch, grasp any form of clay I can to make a vessel.

Down

I fold my black bathing suit
over the bathroom rail to dry,
its outline on the bright towel
like an animal skinned, summer over.

The frost wraps each blade of grass
as if in plastic to store until spring.
The maple's golden leaves about
to skitter the sky, dance a trance,

dervish, until landing. Not an en masse
effort. Rather, as if death can only
come after each moment, so bright,
so light, finds its own winsome way down.

Medals

Each pane in my 1814 saltbox
is filled with autumn's colours,
like a religious stain glass window.

And as if it is shattered, pieces
fall to the ground outside. Life not
so perfectly arranged. Yet, trunks

of oaks, ash, maple stand like
attendant soldiers. Have thrown down
one year's medals, just to earn more.

Kaleidoscope

The spindly geranium stalks in the front containers,
are like the broken threads for a loose button,

hard to keep summer intact. The fall has become
gold-leafed, bits chip away like off a Rembrandt

masterpiece. In winter we forget such splendor
except when we build a fire and it burns into tips

like a flaming maple leaf. Remember the cold of
forgetting, the sharp etching of a blank space

until we recall autumn's kaleidoscope of colour,
rearranging itself like memories collide inside

with a different pattern imprinted, today, yesterday,
tomorrow, telescoping how we see the moment.

In Your Face

This is death in your face,
leaves, darkened and papery
left in the trees, like pamphlets
to convert the passerby to its

dire theory. Military flags at
the cemetery, like this is out
and out war, the struggle. Snow
will cover everything, mummify

the landscape, make it full of
scrawny hieroglyphics on a pyramid's
wall, and when we struggle to
decipher it, we will be, in fact, buried.

In Between

Mums remain stoic, bright, a pot of gold
at the end of summer's rainbow when
falling leaves will bleed red, yellow,
orange into a luminous one arced at

our doorstep. It is the in between
of November and early December
which takes the most faith, trees
likes actors backstage, wait for

their next costume, and for sleet
to hold a sheet up to guard modesty.
In January, we rethink roles, shaken in
our own bubble, blurry as a snow globe.

A Message

But the turkey isn't grateful!
I email a friend who sends
an image of one with a message
of thanks! His spread of feathers

like the first father's collars
setting them off in portraits.
Always a bit grim as if they
had to swallow a bitter pill.

Head truncated from body,
like I daresay today's celebrated
bird, and like we lose ours as
we overeat and by the anesthetizing

of our brain, become as dumb
as one. The turkey, a metaphor
for stuffing, the fat feed of
food, as it says: *Gobble! Gobble!*

Position

Sugar maple leaves bright as lemons trees
in the dark gloom of a Tuscany eve,
where the Cyprus stand like wicks

blown out. The downed brown foliage
everywhere, stubbed in sidewalk cracks.
Torn bits of a paper bag, the trunks finally

fought out of. The pink of Dogwood,
ballet tulles with awkward limbs underneath,
wait for the season to change position.

No One Here to Tell

Dust to Dust

I visit your grave where brown curled
maple leaves hover, are a flock of spring

sparrows, cover you with feathers.
The November landscape, full of dead plants,

droop like untied shoe laces. The world opens
with a sky inviting us into the unknown.

A blue tarp tent held by spikey trees where we
dwell in a child's drawing. A BBC Radio

programme on moon astronauts said the earth
is a spaceship travelling an unknown location.

Here we are passengers unable to fall off,
stuck like cloves in a Christmas Orange,

barely notice the heavens' swirl, we're rockets
heads up, unable to lift. Yet, I, who fear

heights know, as I lay down to be a snow
angel, flap the cold. A white summer moth

stuck on its back, the lights above scattering
the dark is the bright dust from whence I came.

No One Here to Tell

The deer and her doe leaped onto
Wykeham Road from out of spring
woods, as if trying to clear the yellow
line's rainbow. Airborne and sudden.

That the coffee plunger's ring
fell off when I pushed it down,
and careened sideways, like
a wooden cart wheel in mud season.

That a widow told me never
to buy a gaggle of bananas now
that I am alone. They all ripen
at once, fingers in too many pies.

Neither

It isn't like your tombstone
is the hatchet blade that buried you,
come un-hinged from the force of resistance.

Neither is it when shadowed at twilight,
the hang man's black head mask with
the tip disguising who pushes the lever.

But see it more like a marker for
a car parked, I can't pretend you
can back out of, turn the wheel around.

Envelope

The top of the gravestone points up,
stands like an envelope with the flap
opened, below it shadows into an
oblong shape as if death has written me

a letter. I know the contents as I sit in
my Jag, window down, and note the maple
is full blown green. Will send missives
come Fall down on your site, answer

back that life has been sweet, and bright,
full of nuance as every leaf tells,
before it curls up like an Egyptian scroll,
then becomes the dust of the desert.

I think of the tips of the pyramids,
their geometric mountains of precision,
slaves like ants at work carry anything
in to fill the void. Packed for the pharaoh's

journey, a time capsule of a life. I fold
a cotton handkerchief into a triangle, place it
in your jacket pocket, make death gentlemanly,
so you can wipe your brow after a long trip.

This Land

I think of your body like
an anchor. Coffin, a ship,
rocks in the grain of its sea.

Cradle for your dreams,
a music box I still hear,
a weight lowered to hold

me where the roads of
this land are like my heart,
cracked open by memory.

The fault lines like a spindly
vine reaching to attach,
as if I was just planted here.

Reign of Gold

The sun wants its reign of Gold.
Effigies burnt everywhere as trees
ghost out in red, yellows, oranges.

It wants to imitate the rain's intimate
downpour, feeling the world with long
fingers. Follow the snow's option to cover up

the earth, tuck it in under sheets for
winter's long rest. The sun wants us to comb
out its golden locked hair as we rake

lawns, mothers getting rid of snags. It
yearns that we pat the leaves, hold them
like souvenirs before they disintegrate, crumble.

Lights

My flashlight's round beam with a dot in the middle,
is an eye, with a pupil, blind seeing me through the dark

as I walk from the kitchen door to the woodpile.
The full moon has slipped down through the labyrinth

of maple trees, cast a tangled shadow as if the boughs
are trying to hold onto it. Inside the fire leaps up against

the logs laid down like the coffin lid on your tomb.
A week after your funeral the mortician sent a bill

for $200 more to cover your full burial. How can I
tally a price to bury your memory, have it be still, rest?

Gravestones

Death is grave as theses stones
attest, stand like grey flannelled soldiers.

None, out of step, with military flags
here and there. Face East at attention.

To receive the sun's gold rimmed bugle call.
Its light reads each tomb like a found dog tag.

Early Tombstones

Blunt, un-fancy, as if death
is factual, decent, un-adorned.

So, I select a plain headstone,
it shoulders the sky like the cardboard

in set for your dry-cleaned shirts,
the process of death as penetrating.

Solidly etched where a widow
blinded by grief can read the braille

of letters with her fingers. Hug
the stone like a dead husband's torso.

No One Visits

No one visits their dead.
tombstones, a reminder of
Moses' slab of laws brought
to and stuck in earth.

A personal wailing wall
where tears might soften
words carved in the testimonial
to the beloved's death.

A name left to the elements,
seasons erase like from a child's
school tablet, because the numbers
written down don't add up.

Solid

The wilted daffodil, a pinched
flame, melted yellow candle
wax drips on the side of the road

into the cemetery. Where
one red, and one white upside
down paint can mark where

your headstone will go like
party hats. A one foot metal
marker with orange plastic

ribbon flows from each corner
of the spot, sparkles welcome
a Christening in reverse. A name

not given watering the bud of
a baby's head, but one weighted,
down, made solid, etched with a life.

No Life is Set in Stone

No life is set in stone,
but here your birth and
death are solidly engraved.

I visited your burial site,
with grass slightly indented,
lines of your plot as if you

were just here. An intimate
spot, where a widow talked
in private. Now a tombstone

makes your absence public,
a road sign of your passing,
a law etched on a tablet.

Severed

The three trees, one oak, one maple, one ash
severed in the cemetery leave rings
of time, an axe stilled with its furious

hand, cutting into the inner circles like
a phonograph arm into a rotating L.P.
And as the dead want shade too, the shadow

of a branch is an arm playing the harp
of their headstone, with the nuance
of silent music. And I imagine from

heaven where saints are all brightness,
they too might want the remembrance
of the struggle of dark and light across

their etched name, before they too fell,
like a tree, the wind blew through, the sun
touched, and the rain trembled leaves.

Effigy

When I hurl the large black
plastic garbage bags into
the dumpster, they mimic
clouds of smoke over
a cremation burial site.

Heavy to carry, for a moment
airborne, light as memories
fly before they land. The fire
I made this morning, a red
passionate mouth, so eager too,

to take you back as I burn
debris from your life. Ash to
ashes, our shadow, an imprint
of a charred body, an effigy
the light of our days consumes.

Pitch

Gravestones on the Washington Green,
make the cemetery appear roomy, a display
of headstands for beds in a capacious

furniture store. Each one like the door
to the tomb Christ broke open. A gate into
the blue summer drift of an afternoon sky.

Tombstones, Christ Church, Warwick,
the blade in a cricketer's bat which cannot
forever deflect the pitch of the sun's ball.

Tooth Fairies

How can death be made new,
but here your tombstone
boasts of it, as if just fresh minted.

I watched your coffin go
down into earth, a treasure
chest full of the riches of you.

Hidden there, like my secret,
your whereabouts otherwise
unknown. The earth and I

conspiring to tuck you
safely away. Now I know
this place is but a marker,

where the angels came
like tooth fairies hovering
over the stubbed fang

of your gravestone. Came,
wings, fountains spouting
water, to soften hard ground.

Clumsy

The tombstone to the right of the North Door
at Christ Church looks like a mummy, white,
thinnish, a Papier Mache job, similar to ghost
ornaments made for the Day of the Dead, Mexico.

Not evocative of ones airborne, but rather one
taking a rest. An odd shaped creation, made
by an amateur's hand, like wrapping a body
in bedsheets, then plunking it down on the earth.

One imagines it coming undone, unravelling bones
obscured, a napkin releasing cutlery. Whitewash lumpy,
a gone wrong, sugary Advent sweet. Nothing fancy to
the form, clumsy and seemingly rushed, as death often is.

About the Author

Nancy Anne Miller is a Bermudian poet with eight books: *Somersault* (*Guernica Editions* CA 2015), *Because There Was No Sea* (Anaphora Literary Press USA 2014), *Immigrant's Autumn* (Aldrich Press USA 2014), *Water Logged* (Aldrich Press 2016), *Star Map* (FutureCycle press 2016), *Island Bound Mail* (Kelsay Books 2017), *Boiling Hot* (Kelsay Books 2018), *Tide Tables* (Kelsay Books 2019). Her poems have appeared *in Edinburgh Review (UK), Agenda (UK),Ambit (UK), Stand (UK),The International Literary Quarterly (UK), Magma (UK), Journal of Postcolonial Writing (UK),Wasafiri(UK), adda (UK), Mslexia (UK), New Welsh Review (UK), The Moth (IE),A New Ulster (IE), Poetry Ireland Review (IE) Dodging The Rain (IE), Southword Journal (IE), SurVision (IE), The Fiddlehead (CA), The Dalhousie Review (CA),The Toronto Quarterly blog (CA), Postcolonial Text (CA), Transnational Literatures (AU),The Caribbean Writer (VI), tongues of the ocean (BS),Sargasso: Journal of Caribbean Literature (PR), Bim (BB), Poui (BB), PREE (JA), Moko: Caribbean Arts and Letters (TT),Commentaries(MF), The Arts Journal (GY) The Pacuare Anthology (CR), Metaphor (PH), The Missing Slate (PK), The Open Road Review (IN),The Taj Mahal Review (IN),The Punch Magazine (IN), Papercuts (IN), Poetry Salzburg Review (AT), BM Publishers (ZA),Proud Flesh: New Afrikan Journal of Culture, Politics, Consciousness USA), Journal of Caribbean Literatures (USA), Anthurium: A Caribbean Studies Journal(USA), St. Katherine's Review (USA), Hampton Sydney Poetry Review(USA), Theodate (USA) Free Verse: A Journal of Contemporary Poetry and Poetics* (USA), *Interviewing the Caribbean* (USA), among others. She has an M. Litt. in Creative Writing from Univ. of Glasgow, is a MacDowell Fellow, and is a three-time recipient of Bermuda Art Council Grants. She represented Bermuda in Poetry World Cup, organized Ber-Mused, a poetry reading for BDA's 400th Anniversary in 2009. She was shortlisted for the small axe salon (Caribbean) poetry prize (2013), guest-edited *tongues of the ocean (BS)*, for a *Bermuda* edition, and was included in *Arts Etc. Barbados'* (BB) tribute for Edward Kamau Brathwaite.